T0124132

MONKSWEAR

MONKSWEAR
PAUL QUENON

FONS VITAE

First published in 2008 by
Fons Vitae
49 Mockingbird Valley Drive
Louisville, KY 40207
http://www.fonsvitae.com
Email: fonsvitaeky@aol.com

Copyright Fons Vitae 2008

Library of Congress Control Number: 2008922430

ISBN 1-891785-15-X

No part of this book may be reproduced
in any form without prior permission of
the publishers. All rights reserved.

This book was typeset by Neville Blakemore, Jr.

Printed in Canada

I would like to thank Marty Gervais, who suggested I write about things closer to home. What is closer than the clothes on my back? Also I thank John B. Lee and Robert J. Hill for editorial suggestions, and also for his collaborative work on the photography. Thanks also to Jeff Giraldo for collaborative camera work. Finally, thanks to Mike Bevers for proofreading and sensitive editing.

Table of Contents

Table of Contents, continued

From The Call of Wild Geese,
"All Soul's Day"

Now we have our brief moment here.
We came yesterday, are here today,
will be gone tomorrow.
Let that brief moment be spent in communion
with the whole of life
so that we will not have lived in vain.

Father Matthew Kelty, OCSO
Monk of Gethsemani

Dad's Ash Tray

God's image remains within you
even though you superimpose upon it
the earthly likeness of the man of dust...
                                    Origen

Round brass rim with black char in the middle,
the only shiny thing in the living room.

Dusty-golden with three notches in it,
a smudge in the middle, rough to the touch.
Afterwards my fingers did not taste good.

It arrived as a gift
from Dad's office,
pure gold maybe, or as good as.
A surprise gift.

In the center, I saw my face golden.
My twin too saw my face,
but I did not see hers.
How come? A magic bowl.

Then he spoiled it
knocked his pipe down
against the shiny tray
and left all that blackness.

In my infant curiosity
I went to find my face
touched the tarnished rim
and dumped ashes on the carpet.

I was told not to touch again,
~the only shiny thing in the room.
Then my hand was roughly wiped clean.

Why anyone would want
to keep ashes I did not understand.
You couldn't eat them.

Scrub it hard, my brother says,
it'll be shiny gold again.
Scrub hard. No one does.

It sits, a sallow gold frame
around an opaque mirror.
So it stays that way.

***

My twin and I, old enough to walk,
were put in the play pen for nap time,
with some boring toys
good for nothing but
for throwing outside the pen.

Then she cried and said she wanted Dolly here.
So repentant, I devised to climb
for the very first time ever,
over the wooden pen bars,
brought the toy back, and climbed back in.

Then I saw the ash tray - the golden dish,
the irresistible shiny thing in the room.
And no one here but us two...

The Devil's Going To Get You

—our big brothers tell us.
It might be true, since
the devil's face is right there,
painted on the coal-bin door.

Sure enough, just when
Mom & Dad were away,
a stomping came from the basement,
a chanting, clomping up
the stairs, booming voices:
The **De**-vil's
go'ng- to
get-you!

I knew of their plot already
but behind my hilarity
it sounded almost convincing.
I was afraid to let myself believe...

My sister, terrified,
ran upstairs where her big sister
quickly wised her up
and spoiled our fun.

To this day I am left
with an exquisite taste
for make-believe
that is really real
if you get it,
walking in procession,
chanting with fifty Brother
Monks. Were I afraid
to let myself believe
it was really Jesus coming
maybe it wouldn't be.

The Novice Cloak

—a hooded full length wrap
with front flap
from neck to foot.

On my birthday, a month
after receiving the cloak
I drew a card for my twin sister.
Then
regretted what I saw.
Me, all cloth, peering out
from inside the hood
sitting sad faced,
I wanted her to see
I was happy.
No revisions
produced a happy face
nearly as convincing
as the sad one.

After 10 years
and Solemn Vows
the cloak gave place
to the cowl:
a body tent
spreading as one air pocket
from peak to ground.

Good for sitting out in the cold
meditating, with sleeves,
wide generous sleeves,
crossed over my knees
draped to the feet.
A tent to pray in.

Cold weather meditation
Method: sit tall
hood up
7 layers of warmth
over the knees:
trousers, robe,

scapular, cowl
four layers of sleeve cloth
—seven altogether.
Snuggle hands through
slits alongside the pockets
warm on knees.
Good enough for 20 degrees,
10, 5, less...

For half an hour I sit content,
tented with the
Indwelling Presence.

From beneath
an overhanging roof
I peer out
 —not sad faced—
and watch the cope
of the enveloping sky.

Dear Eileen:
It's cold and lonely here.
I like it that way.

Happy Birthday.

Ash Wednesday

A coal black char-cross,
is generously smeared
on each shaved head
front to back, side to side
—no subtlety about it.

Remember, Paul
you are coal dust...
back home in coal country
soot in the air,
caked up nostrils
lodged under fingernails.

Kids, don't track up,
don't go near the coal bin.
Dad made sure of that,
painted a Devil on
the coal-bin door.

We heard Jews were
shoveled into a furnace.
We heard: Be good
or the Devil will put you
into the furnace.

My big brothers invited
my twin sister and me
down to see the devil.
I quietly descended behind her.
Just when she saw it, I yelled
clutched her shoulders and
she began to cry

terribly.

Even into adult years she would
blame me about that. Who knows?
perhaps she *did* see the Devil.

Remember Paul
you are ash
and ashes are
no joke.

My Scapular

Dark crow wings
two black swatches
front and back
stretched down
over head, heart,
belly, loins
to just below
the knees.

A crow never migrates.
He hangs around all winter,
hollers at the cold
and flaps off to where
the rest of the gang
is making enough of a ruckus
to kill off winter
'til spring seeps in.

A "murder" of crows
they're called.

Every day I lift and
drop over my head
this black flutter of
fabric and hurry off
to crowd in
the echoey choir
where enough a
row is made
to melt the icy
core belted beneath
my scapular which
chants
in its rough
heated crow way

Nevermore,
icy core
saying:
Nevermore

Nevermore.

A lonely crow joins
a loud, cursing, cruising flock
crazy for the cold.

Hair Off

On the streets of 2004
hair off
is in, and
hair on is
out.

Since monks
swear
to be out
should monks
wear
hair on?

No, change
never ends
and soon again
I will be
out
on my head
not a hair
in my head
not a thought.

The Hood

—a hiding place
for the head

a portable anonymity

a refuge from
artificial light

a cover to make
dimness dimmer

to make time
slow down

to make ready
for the rain

for the rain that will come.

Under this thin
black fabric
I brood long
slow and steady

a yes,
an un-
qualified
yes

against that day
that downpour of
no
       no
  no
that will surely come

Then I will slip
my hood back and
let my old white head
shine with a
pure, unqualified

yes.

Hair-cutting Day In An Eighteenth Century Print

Hair-cutting comes once a month
according to the Usages. Everyone
gets shaved on the same day.

Three monks sit attended by
two Laybrothers and one Choir Monk.
A novice waits nearby reading a book,
with his hood up against the air
coming through a half open window.
His cold feet hug one another.
He wears wooden shoes with
up-turned toes, as do the others.
A large key dangles from his belt strap,
for even in monasteries
a door must be locked.

One burly barber with a blacksmith's paw
delicately supports a flat razor with
his little finger. His speechless lips sag,
he gazes pensively down his massive nose
attending to the almost sleeping head
of a white-beard…with fingers interlocked on his lap.

Beside him, with hands placidly folded,
a Brother rests with his thoughts,
lips—a thin down-curved line
as he appraises a crop failure.
His dark half bald head
is guided lightly by the priest,
whose own side fringes
remain to be cut.

A frail senior sits with infinite patience,
head tilted slightly, face worn sensitive
to every whiff of sin and infidelity
in God's precious garden.

Down the shadowed stairway
descends a Brother with book in tow.
Up on the wall hangs a small shrine

of some hooded saint who
stretches compassionate hands
down to this quiet brood of
the blessedly mournful.

A Twentieth Century Photograph
of Hair-cutting Day.

Seated on a line of stools, three monks
gaze beyond the picture's edge.
While their coronas are carefully trimmed
they watch some calves on the hillside.

Along a bench ~ a clutter of scissors,
whisk brushes and electric clippers.
Across the far wall, sweat filled
work blouses air out.
Two priests in denim clothes
are tying their shoes.
One stooped senior with a cane
has risen to leave, replaced by another
being draped with a blur of a cloth.

A barber, his lean wrist poised with a comb,
peers intently through wire-rimmed spectacles
at a white head with a homebody face,
droopy eyes and a button-mushroom lip.
He is in a revery over the certain joy
of his way-side garden coming to bloom.

Another, with a round face,
is calmly settled in a level gaze.
A deep crescent shadow sculpted
by his shaven head curves
down to the tip of his bushy eyebrow.
His penetrating mind
rests simple, innocent
and empty in the quiet flurry
of this moment.

The moment peels away.
They rise, shake hair off the cloths
and depart. The moment has traveled
forty years and now lies
printed on a leaf inside this book
on my lap. Just beyond
the photo's right edge,

descending the whitewashed, mildewed
stairway, my wiry twenty-something frame
enters the musty Parlor and sits
just as the photographer leaves.

Donning the Cowl

..is like fighting a sail
made of 4 yards of cotton.

My first try:
hold collar with one hand
with other hand
gather hem
up to neck
swing it round
over head and
drop-release
over body
in one
flop.

Bad try! I'm
smothered and blinded.

Improved method:
Gather hem to collar,
first fit around neck
then drop-release the rest.
Punch out long, impossibly
long billowy sleeves.
Then with nifty flick
of wrists heft up
excess cloth
clear your hands
lower hood, straighten tip
with arm in Full Nelson
twist behind.

Then briskly step
to the next
prayer-attack on
God in church.

Method of doffing:
The stalwart Richard
striding down the cloister

gathers the length
up to neck
lifts overhead, off and
flips down the
fabric with a
thwack.

Tossing it on shoulder
he swings wide
a door and is

vanished.

Cincture:

a careworn strip of leather
circling round my waist
and drooping off my left hip
half way to the floor.

The trailer splits double:
a forked tongue
of the serpent that
never left us.
It rides my hips
and clutches my guts
until the grave swallows
us both.

One of seven
knot-lumps holds the belt-
slit fast, that slips
outward or in
as the body swells
or withers with
creeping mortality.

This hide strip of one dead cow
still yields with every breath I take
of sweet-stink from
a distant herd
heaving out loud complaints
of relentless desire.

Fossils of cattle longing
creep in every cell
belting my waist and
plunge off my hip to
reach the ground never,

ever to dangle
a swaying tail
a ceaseless twitch
that sinks to my quick
until the day I am
unquickened.

I retire at night
and with one easy sweep
I unfasten and hang
limp the old one-eyed trooper
on a hook

     for the night

until rising in the dark
and taking a breath
I hitch him back on
and stride off again
to Vigils.

Shrewdness of the Snake

Taste death.
It's the spice
of life.

Know evil
or you will never
know good.

Acquire acumen
the ache of critical doubt.

Stand back
separate now from
your own soul.

Doubt everything
but your own
doubt.

Are you feeling
naked? Are you
growing numb?

Why the commandments?
To learn in so many ways
How to love myself.

Wisdom of the Serpent

Let void
be pivot
to All.

Know
the nought
of knowledge.

Be bliss,
acknowledgment
of being.

Now
who are you?
what is paradise?

Is there any
difference?

Monk's Cassock

I stand a man of the cloth
—and plenty of it—
hidden inside a steam pressed
cotton tunic snappered up
to a prim collar which stands
one inch high
—sanitary, bloodless
washable, white for me
washed clean in
the blood of the Lamb—
a pretty pricey item!

On either side
pockets of inexhaustible depth.
Magic pockets!
I have to lean sideways
to reach bottom.
Contents on the right:
handkerchief, penlight
Swiss Army knife,
chapping lotion
pitch pipe, rosary.
Left side: keys, dental
floss, notes to be
discarded, eyeglasses.
Pockets deep enough
to smuggle two wine bottles
right through the cloister.

The Laundry Number

—patched inside the back collar
of each cowl and scapular is
a designated number
to sort out in the wash
whose is which and
what goes where.

Above each patch is
a loop that hangs on a peg.
Number, loop, peg—
a hanging cipher
for an unnamed person
who wears thin, wears
habitually the same habit
over and over
and owns not a stitch,
not a loop, not
a number, owns not
his very own body
even

even as he is
a God-owned body
in a God-owned garb
which hangs on a loop
in a row of pegs
a voiceless choir
answering each
to that high Ledger
where after the great
wash and agitation
the heat and pressure
that Searching Hand
will then sort out
who is who
and who belongs where
and will lift up and carefully
place each one
onto his own
designated
peg.

The Jolly Gravedigger

for Br. Michael Ingram

The day before a funeral
a groaning dinosaur
has invaded the cemetery.
A backhoe is efficient
but indelicate. I keep my distance.
A hand hewn grave brings monks
together as we open
a nothing where something was.
Characters with grudges
grow affable, and the affable
grow hilarious.

Such was young Brother Michael:
after the community dispersed
and the crew was filling the grave
his wit grew sharper and
echoes of laughter bounced
around the cemetery walls.
Indelicate perhaps,
or a rare realism that well
suits our bare earth burials
without coffin or vault
to keep out rain and
other earthly visitors.

Always accident prone,
Michael fell to his death
constructing a studio.
When they carried his bier
into church, his young face wore
a gleaming smile, later sealed
to a tight lipped propriety.

At the visitors' grief
the rotund belly of
the sage Fr. Roger tightened
with a suppressed laugh,
as if he knew some secret
hidden from the world,

yet shared with
The Resurrection Kid
laughing over the handle
of his shovel, packing down
a treasure where there was none.

Saint Levi

"Follow me."

That's all he said.
No whereto. No why.

Anything more
would have caused
suspicion.

So I followed—

the easiest thing
in the world

to fall
so
low

at the tug
of my deepest

freedom.

The Ladder of Humility

We ascend this ladder
by descending —Rule of St. Benedict

Walking is
just a continual
falling and
catching yourself
as you fall again
below that high
which caught you
on your last fall

falling over
the curved globe
which always
drops lower
every step you take,
like the Little Prince
on his Little Planet
the horizon always
drops even if
on Big Planets
you have to climb
to get there.

Every fall
puts you
on top of the world
until the next fall
puts you on top
again.

Straw Mattress

A sturdy duck-cloth case
was tightly stuffed, sealed,
punctured and buttoned flat—
a unique smell of straw
and flax, a few seeds caught
in the weave. When sat upon
it yielded a muffled crunch
but little comfort. In a year it
sank to the shape of the body.

Every autumn mattresses were
lugged outside to air out sweat,
returned and flipped over
to its flatter side. Mine was
second hand, had dips and peaks
in the wrong places, as if
I must conform to the shape
of an anonymous someone,
conform to any monk through
years of living together
always, in the church, scriptorium,
refectory, fields, Grand Parlor,
shaped, punched, re-shaped,
softened to a dough—until
you find your own hard bones
that will make someone else yield.

In these latter days, I sleep under
the open sky as my dormitory,
shaping myself to every new
climate and constellation as
the year moves on—waking face
to face with Hercules, Leo, Orion,
each one aloof, silent, each an enigma
making its own ancient, anonymous imprint.

Possessed By A Habit

Sorry, but I can't seem to shed
this habit I'm so given over to,
this monkwear, this second skin
I'm so habituated to.

I've worn it till the habit has
worn me quite down
to a shadow of the man
I once was. You would
hardly recognize the boy
who at least had *some* promise
and risked talents, life and
opportunities for the sake
of a possessive, chronic
habit which he won't shake off,
that holds him so hide-bound
he has all but lost
everything

which seems to be
the way he wants it
given the merry way
he carries on with
no thought of past,
future, or of what
might become of him
once he wakes up
and finds himself without
means or ability
to sustain so religiously
his mystifying
habit!

Just you see—unless
he quits this habit it will eventually
carry him to the grave.

Amen, Alleluia!

Dear-End Prayer While Using Beads

I grab my beads as rescue from sleep
•
and push beads along without words
•
at least to touch is something
•
a touch, a faint hint of a word *Lord, Jes...*
•
Just to keep going if not praying.
•
I think of St. Teresa with her irresistible raptures,
•
and Carmelites who wonder
why they don't have irresistible raptures
•
who sink like me ~ I like them.
•
I pull my head up, *have mercy,*
breathe, aware I'll come
•
to the last bead before
•
the dead-end knot where I'm
left holding the string

and nowhere to go,
except back

•

to the last bead *...me a sinner,* after
•
I prepare, breathe, almost undrench from sleep
•
being not even like Carmelites
•
wondering why they don't have
•
St. Teresa's irresistible
raptures, ones

I think about while
•
I barely keep going
•
with some faint brush of a word
•
and a touch at least of bone-beads
•
pushing along with scarcely a prayer
•
grabbed for rescue from
dead-end sleep.

My prayer sloughs along
Slumps to a stop, 'til a wren
Ring, rings me awake.

Discretion

en gastri ekei
Is. 7:14
Mt. 1:23

Hardly anything less
could be said,
and that already
too much.
(in the "tummy"
she "will have")

best leave the rest
unsaid.

"I was carrying then..."
—Josephine, my mother—
for my child ears
no what, no where
best not hear
body parts, if
mentioned at all
left vaguely regional

such as "gastri"
belly—too vulgar
tummy—too cute
stomach—too precise
womb—ditto

let's say
she will be *carrying*

and so we would,
save for Elizabeth
who blurted out
"Blessed the fruit
of your *womb*!"

And now in prayer
over and over
century after century
the one most named body part
of anyone on earth
on the lips of numberless children!

47

Moon eclipsed to red.
It's time to write a letter
to a long lost friend.

In a Garden of Lies

for Marty Gervais

Plato, as you know, Marty
wanted to kick poets out of town.
for being such liars!

Monks flee the cities
to get away from lies.
So why does a poet like you
leave town and come to the monastery?
It makes me wonder.

I, myself, instinctively mistrust
whoever swears up and down
they are telling the solemn truth.
You swear up but not down
you are professionally telling lies.
So maybe I half-way trust you.
At least you keep truth on a human scale.

God alone
in our oblique theology
tells lies on a grand scale.
Every word and event a
disguise of the Unpronounceable.

I turn the leaves of
your latest volume rich with
act-dumb complacency
over what, ultimately,
neither one of us
has yet to see.

Better to keep it that way, Marty.
Better to keep it that way.

Mountain Climb

I set out alone towards the east,
walking in a summer afternoon
on a secret trail through
a grassy forgotten valley
and find my way to a mountain
that no one knows about.
I have been here before,
explored alone the route
that only I know. It is very familiar
though changed—
always familiar, though
never twice the same.
I have the energy
to take the long irregular climb.

I arrive at the summit
totally alone. Something absolute
grips my senses. I all but breathe it in.
I have been here, I know
I have been here before.

The descent glides past
a wooded meadow
to the monastery, where
I will be happy to show
it to others.

I awake.
It is dark.
My sense of the summit
begins to fade, as always.
But this time I will
help it stay.

I walk it in the dark.
Alone, after Laud,
towards wintry hills,
distant silhouettes,
confident on the pale road
in the memory,

—the summit beyond no more
than shadow and sky.

It is enough.

A Mala Round My Neck

First seen thrown on a shelf
        by a friend back from Tibet.
My curiosity was rewarded
        by its bestowal around my neck,
        with scarcely an introduction.

I still hardly know this near-by stranger from afar
        who carries my invocations
        on Yak bone up the heights
        packing along
        Lord have mercy

one hundred bones, with eight extra
        for wayward thoughts
a long caravan
        sandstone to touch
        studded turquoise
        mountain sky
        studded
        Son of the Living God

each bloody with carnelian
        on me a sinner

copper banded
        Lord Jesus
                silver banded
                        Christ, Son...
finger polished, green stained

pushed along a leather string
        one after one, plodding
have mercy on us
        have mercy on...

The Day the Airplanes Did Not Fly

No trailers
scored the blue

no mute rumble
rolled through

air blue as
the Age of Innocence

No flashers
passed stars

in stillness deep
as night
long before
Cain slew
Abel

Briefly learned we
how once
the world was we've
uncreated

learned and waited in
that dark shell
~ horror

Star Sailors

I awake at 2:55, and gaze
at the perfectly cloudless sky.
My eye drifts, then returns
to a star I should have noticed,
magnitude 3rd or 2nd. I stare awhile.
It fades to half brightness,
then vanishes.
Star-sailors? The space station
revolving, that briefly reflects
the hidden sun then turns?

Yesterday morning, at Mass,
an image came,
out-spread bodies free-falling
through the air over streets
of New York City—
and a question:
Perhaps some of them knew
exhilaration as the last seconds
stretched—stretched before
the instant end?

Later that day while I worked
on BxWs in the darkroom,
a woman's voice came over the radio:
Contact with the space shuttle Columbia
has been lost. A silent pause, and then
a man's voice: The shuttle Columbia
has vanished. Multiple trailers
were seen in the sky.

Did some of them know exhilaration
before their brief end?

The following night I dream:
the suspended gear
of an optometrist
swings before my face.
Penetrating light
painfully probes

the root of my vision
I breathe deeply, shed a tear,
stare into the core of that orb
and see cross-hairs, Cruciform.

In the darkroom of deep space,
light from a shutter opened briefly.
The Shuttle's raw exposure
burned on this darkened land
an indelible print.

Weird Arithmetic

The middle cipher
In the word God is zero.
In the word good

stands zero x zero.
Naught times naught
equals all nothings lodged

in God's open heart

Primal Prayer

A bomb falls in Baghdad.

A child dies in Baghdad.
Another child lives.

A bomb falls and explodes.
Another child is born
and dies.

Would I had the voice of an infant
I would wail.
An infant wail cannot say yes
cannot say no.
Only my infant wail
would touch
Your Holiness.

Only the infant wail
is truth.

Nothing's in My Name

My senior monk, Fr. Kneckt
was a servant
in name and spirit.

Surely, Br. Armour
is love at work,

And Br. Monarch:
an aristocrat so
humble in these latter days.

But what in the world
is a Quenon?

A *What Not*—
que non—
in the Latin
feminine form.
Perhaps
the very Mother of
possibilities!

a *what-not* of whatever.

Or am I rather a chip
off the old Greek
kenos—emptiness—*kenon*
in the accusative
where I stand
accused as

a nothingness
manifest in
time and space,

a *nihil* negated—
the original inflation
collapsed to particulate
somethingness.

A thisness
devoid of being,

an indefinite cipher
stripped to
the primordial

mothering
naught

as

Quenon

My Long Tail

What is the significance of...?

Inevitably visitors ask
about the long tail on my belt
a yard of superfluous leather.
They sometimes think
I am the Abbot because
my tail is so long, or I'm
advanced in status,
someone enlightened.

My utilitarian answer:
it's something obsolete.
It could hitch the cowl
behind the back while
washing hands or making a bed.
No one, anymore
would make a bed in their cowl,
or even, maybe, make their bed.

I am a vanishing species
with a dangerous tail
apt to get caught in the car door,
a Doberman they didn't dock.
a horse like John Henry whose
14 foot of tail fit his fame for arrogance.
I stride with tail swinging free
annoying the practical minded
in their mail-order belts
who believe in nothing insignificant.

My significance is
I am no more significant
than neck ties or coat lapels
or studs on a belt.
In an age where hat or shirt is
a walking billboard
for Nike or Bud Light
I reserve the privilege
to be a mountain ram with

a head of French Horns
a puffin with axe-head beak
a peacock trailing a Persian carpet

I remain a freak of natural excess,
a side track of evolution,
a question for the archeologist
of the human dig who
will pick me up, look me over
and fail to figure out:
What's the significance of that?

Kindly Folk All

Many thoughtful people
out in the e-mail world
believe it very, very important
that I take Viagra. I hear from them
every day.

The discreet Dolly Garland
in carefully coded language,
instructed me on
"What is G. E. N. ERIC VI.A?"
Should my neighbor, Br. Chrysostom
glance at my screen
he'll then think it's about some Eric fellow.

The real hombre Ricardo Cortez
warmly supports my need.
The prim Allie Hinson,
the doubtlessly gorgeous Vanessa Tuffle,
the exotic Lula Pratt,
even Anastasia Hare—
a school Sister I guess—
all surround me with encouragement.

Angela Bartly considerately notifies
"Re: Status of Your Account"
—an account I didn't know I even had!
The meticulous Beth Perez then reminds me
"Please Confirm."
The evangelical Ann Battes proclaims
"Attention to All Men!"
Jarvis Byrd offers me,
in good holiday spirits
80% discount at Christmas time.

Perhaps I am seriously missing out
in the brotherhood of
the avuncular
Heriberto Hampton
the burly Malcom Ruffin
and frolicksome Vito Head.

Meanwhile something called
Pop-up Stopper
has just popped up.
—must be a special pill
these kindly folks designed
to keep a pop-up prone
monk like me
down.

Scapulars

White robe
black stripe:
monks

White fur
black stripe:
skunks

From both
best to keep
your distance.

Footwear

When it comes to where
monks contact ground
we're like everyone else—

each one wears something different:

Reebocks, Rockports, Roebucks,
Roughbacks, and utterly predictable
Birkendorfs.

Nike, Easy, Shuffle, Speedy
and the other seven dwarfs.

Thirty years ago
we wore uniform, droll,
black, polished Dr. Scholl's
gotten at a discount
because Doc was father
to a Trappistine.

In Africa I envied
the monks who walked
with feet bare, every pair
as different as hands and heads.

As for stockings,
the glove that fits the foot,
we're different from
most people—we
all wear the same:
white cotton, common issue.

Forty years ago we wore
duck cloth footies,
and separate leggins that
fit below the heel,
held up to the knees
by elastic garters
(elastic was real modern).
Good washable cover
for barnyard and field.

Fifty years ago our shoes
were home made, uncomfortable
until broken in. Old brothers
wore them to a tatter,
could not be parted from,
would rather die in ruined shoes
then be finally buried in new ones,
lying dead, awkward in
unaccustomed footwear,
already strangers to us
ready as bridegrooms
ready for contact
with new grounds.

Buried Flame

O living flame of love
That tenderly wounds my soul
In the deepest center!

St. John of the Cross:

In early half-dark
I pass a smoldering source
of stale smoke smelled

a half mile away—
fuming, room sized volcano
nearing extinction.

Dry, heaped up trash wood
of buried intensity
burning all night long,

one spark on the ground.
I ignore it and walk on.
Nothing there to see,

all smoke, smothered heat,
pale clouds wafting from the core
that took all this while

to hide its fierceness.
Its quiet intensity
returns each wood mote

to the universe.

Since now you are not oppressive
now consummate! If you will.

Under the Crab Cherry

for Br. Harold

When the crab cherry bloomed
stood dazzling in the noon,
when bees their work had done
when rain had come and gone,

blissful petals snowed down
and nested one by one
on his thin tuft of hair
and blessed his quiet dome

wherein, through long decay,
words scrambled, lost in space,
but thought stood still as stone,
he'd found the deep Unknown.

Glimpses of Charles

Such a happy face
Head under earphones
a recording of birdcalls.

Stumbling restlessly
at night in the dorm, mumbling
"that train in Brazil
...off a bridge...killed
three hundred people.."

Folding laundry
laughing at his own jokes.
For the umpteenth
time he imitates
Fr. Leonard's quacky sermon:
"The novices liked
my last one so well
I'll give it again."

Items in his laundry:
One big bright plastic sunflower.
A ponderous dictionary
open on a pedestal,
covered with dust.
A huge enlargement
of The Little Flower
her open face beaming
love enough for
the whole wide world.

Passing a bowl of
Hershey's kisses
he deftly slips a fist
full into his pocket
without a pause.

On 50th anniversary:
"If I had it to do over again
I wouldn't worry so much!"

Elbow on belly
chubby hand on brow
Charles hears Chapter.
Slowly his head sinks,
slowly his hand slides higher
hiding oblivion.

Indian Summer

A cloud cover holds down
a humid blanket of air
against the yellow, brown,
orange, green, red
quilting the hills.

There's a lull in this
migratory season when
the present horizon
is enough—for the present.

It will not remain so,
for the globe travels
and leans away from the sun.

Even the lonely heron
will lift its great blue wings,
rise unseen from Monk's Creek
and turn towards
some remote destination
written invisibly
in its perfect, ancient genes.

You have to slow down
in order to really see
how fast time goes by.

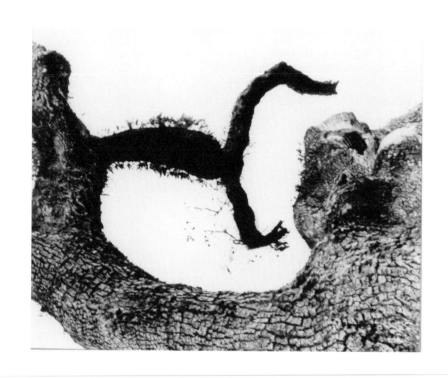

Destiny Whispers

I listened to secrets
the lake-spill was telling
the night; to some lost prayer
swelling the dark breeze;

to Jupiter drawing
closer, night by night to
Scorpio, to unlock
some destiny on earth

that also might strike me
~ death breeds superstition ~
who struck my sister twin
twelve years ago, just when

Jupiter, keyed in line,
gave Scorpio its sting.
Night whispered destiny,
but did not tell it all.

The Farm Truck

A big grey battered 4 wheel drive.
A high ride'n, robust bouncer,
with that Chevy sing.
One dent more is no worry.

The ignition worked without a key.
Who would steal such a wreck?
so we thought.

Rambunctious and unpredictable
it mistook a curve when two farm Brothers
were late for Vespers and ran them
right into a power pole (injuries minor).

A good slam stopped the door rattle.
Dashboard only lit up once speed was gained—
a day laborer, a bull hauler
not a night lifer.

Last month it went missing.
No one had seen it for days,
then weeks. At last it was found
on a ridge 9 miles away
down a holler, burnt
to a crisp, only its square
home-welded bumper
left as proof of identity.

The old trooper on the final
adventure died in a blaze
off a wooded hillside.

No Suspect identified.

Cheesemaking in a 1879 Imprint

Three Laybrothers tend cheese,
each in his own seclusion,
Soft winter light falls steeply
through windows, leaves on the floor
a worker's diffuse shadow.
A small weight and chain clock
marks 1:30 p.m.

A Choir Monk leans back on a counter
with folded arms and head drooping,
—recollected perhaps,
or half asleep in this siesta hour.

One with sleeves rolled up
ladles curds from a vat
into wide wooden flats.
It cools and sets until another
empties them into wooden hoops
placed over cheese cloth, stretched
across vessels where
the whey water drains.

A tall Brother in an apron gently
squeezes down curds
with the large hands of a cow herder

The cheese will set hard overnight,
be lowered by pulley down
the nearby dumb waiter
to the cool basement for aging.
The whey jars perhaps are poured out
for cows from which it came.

Whey is spread on pasture as fertilizer
by monks in the twenty-first century.
Curds are pumped out
a wide hose from an enormous
stainless steel steam vat
into perforated hoops.
In all this heft, plash and uproar
no one stands by half asleep.

Cheese cakes are dunked,
slid down a chute
to chiller vaults,
rolled in salt,
slapped on cypress racks,
dated, cued, aged,
flipped, washed, massaged,
to baby flesh softness.
Each cake carefully handled
dozens of times.

Efficiency's low by today's standards,
a production expert says.

Sodden, soiled, salt is saved
and dumped by the forest
where deer softly come, lower
their muzzles to the ground, taste,
lift their heads, gaze contentedly,
and lower again
knowing nothing of
what century they are in.

take some getting used to,
like the knack of dropping the seat
with no hands, kicking back the bottom edge
to swivel down and catch
with the back of my knee
before it bangs.

White oak, satin to the touch,
adjoining grain in mirror pattern,
about counter-top height,
substantial, bright, roomy.

Quite a change from the looming
dark panels lining the nave walls,
so old the contours of sweaty backs
were slow burned into the varnish,
shadow monks that remained
after the chanters shut the books
and departed.

The floor had worn to shallow troughs
where feet shuffled forward
with each profound bow, then back
to straighten and take in breath
and attack the next psalm, countless
psalms, countless bows
to a slow erosion, a ripple
in the floor boards.

The book ledge frazzled
by small round brass feet
attached to the brass rim
binding enormous antiphonarys
and psalters, each fixed
with two latches that
clattered shut at prayer's end
like a volley of golden bullets
to set the devils a-running.

If the old choir of facing stalls
was a slow barge where we stood
low in its belly, blind in all directions,
the new stalls are power boats
we steer high in open water
and might set a clear course
were it not for the fog
in this new century where
we thought we knew
how to get to where we wanted to go
but are still putting around
taking directions from
some remote navigator
who seems to be
on another ship.

Settling In

They ask: how
longa 'v you been
here? I answer,
like some-other
from elsewhere,
50 years.

But it is a fiction. Time
has shrunk not lengthened.

I used to live by
month and year.
Now if I can bump
through just this week,
I'll leave time
for bells to keep,
and bear a moment
for all its worth.

But sorry, a truckload of time
just came roaring in,
to empty, sort and stack.

How long have I been here?
Excuse me, but I
haven't gotten here yet.

The Cowl

—solemn as chant,
one sweep of fabric
from head to foot.

Cowls hanging
on a row of pegs—
tall disembodied spirits
holding shadows
deep in the folds
waiting for light,
for light to shift
waiting for a bell
for the reach of my hand
to spread out the slow
wings, release the
shadows and envelope my
prayer-hungry body
with light.

The great stone rolled back,
we entered the tomb. Nothing
there but our linens.